# Dear Black Women

AFFIRMATIONS, QUESTIONS, & APOLOGIES YOU MAY NOT HAVE HEARD

D1728099

This book is registered with the Library of Congress.
Copyright ©2021 Jewel Guy & Desmond Guy

All rights reserved. No part of this publication may be reproduced, stored in a retrieval system or transmitted in any manner or by any means without written permission of the author except for brief quotations used for promotion or in reviews.

www.jewelguy.co

*An Ode to Black Women*

*Dear Black Women*
*You are more than enough*
*when the going gets rough*
*it's in You we trust*

*You are hope*
*amongst the desperation*
*You are water*
*fluid in any situation*
*the world's salvation*
*the mother of liberation*

*You are God*
*on this earth*
*the womb from which*
*all life was birthed*
*know Your worth*

*Dear Black Women*
*Forgive our*
*past transgressions*
*the micro aggressions*
*the lack of protection*

*Seeing You*
*not as a supreme being*
*but a mere possession*

*You are more*
*than the circumference*
*of Your behind*
*You are divine*
*One of a kind*
*love sublime*

*By: Desmond Guy*

# A Letter from Jewel Guy

*Dear Black Women,*

Can I be honest? I knew this day would come and for some reason I wasn't looking forward to it. Why not? Simply put, I felt inadequate. Each time a Black woman asked if there would be a book for her, I shrank on the inside. I was immediately filled with doubt and fear of not being able to speak to her situations or needs. This bothered me. However, I understand that fear works to keep us silent. Our fears tell us that we aren't the right person for the job, that no one will understand us, and that we should keep our stories to ourselves. But what would happen if we decided not to give into our fears and share our experiences anyway? Eventually, someone will begin to listen.

When we decided to start writing, I understood almost immediately, that this book would be different. I would finally be standing up for ME. The little girl with the yellow and white romper & red high top tennis shoes, who was fondled by a family member during visits and the frustration & silence that she carried into my adulthood. For my younger self, who battled with anxiety and depression and always wondered if I was good enough. For my teenage self, who while carrying my trauma, moved from relationship to relationship without a clear idea of what I wanted and therefore couldn't communicate my needs. For my adult self, who is learning how to be more aware, compassionate, and loving to myself on this journey called life. It is our shared stories and experiences that bring us together, and with this in mind we offer this book to you.

As you read and work through this book, please know that you are loved, respected, and cherished. My husband has graciously agreed to stand in the gap by providing apologies from a Black man that are long overdue. He pours his love, appreciation, and desire for your healing into every word. You deserve to be safe. You deserve to be heard and understood without judgement. You deserve to heal everything.

# Apologies From A Black Man: Because You Deserve Them

Dear Black Women, Forgive me for treating you as a possession & not a person.

1. Describe a time when you experienced this type of treatment.

_____

_____

_____

_____

2. How did you feel in that situation? How did or does it affect your current interactions with Black men?

_____

_____

_____

_____

3. What do you need to release yourself from the pain caused by these actions?

_____

_____

_____

_____

Dear Black Women, Forgive me for not respecting your right to say "No". I could not handle your rejection.

1. How do you feel when you read this apology?

_____

_____

_____

_____

2. Describe a time when your "No" was not respected. What did you feel in that moment?

_____

_____

_____

_____

3. How has this type of treatment affected the way you interact with Black men?

_____

_____

_____

_____

Dear Black Women, Forgive me for lying to you. I didn't care enough to be honest.

1. Think of a time when you were lied to. How did you feel when someone didn't care enough to be honest with you?

_____

_____

_____

_____

2. How has dishonesty affected your interactions with others?

_____

_____

_____

_____

3. What do you need to release yourself from the pain caused by these actions?

_____

_____

_____

_____

Dear Black Women, Forgive me for breaking your spirit and calling it love.

1. What do you feel when you read this statement?

_____

_____

_____

_____

2. Have you ever received this type of treatment? How did it affect you?

_____

_____

_____

_____

3. What do you need to release yourself from the pain caused by these actions?

_____

_____

_____

_____

Dear Black Women, Forgive me for judging you before making an effort to understand you.

1. When was the last time you felt judged for being YOU?

_____

_____

_____

_____

2. How did you feel in that situation?

_____

_____

_____

_____

3. How did or does judgement from others affect the way you feel about yourself?

_____

_____

_____

_____

Dear Black Women, Forgive me for making you a prisoner of my past, I could only see you through my pain.

1. Describe a time when someone treated you according to their past pain.

_____

_____

_____

_____

2. How did you feel in that situation? How did that affect you?

_____

_____

_____

_____

3. What do you need to release yourself from the pain caused by these actions?

_____

_____

_____

_____

**Dear Black Women, Forgive me for not protecting you. I was only focused on protecting myself.**

1. Describe a time when you needed or desired to be protected by a Black man?

_____

_____

_____

_____

2. How did you feel when protection didn't come?

_____

_____

_____

_____

3. How has that affected you and your interactions with Black men?

_____

_____

_____

_____

**Dear Black Women, Forgive me for not wanting our children, when you no longer wanted me.**

1. What do you feel when you read this statement?

_____

_____

_____

_____

2. Have you experienced this type of disregard after your relationship ended? If so, how has this experience affected you and your child/children?

_____

_____

_____

_____

3. What do you need to release yourself from the pain caused by these actions?

_____

_____

_____

_____

**Dear Black Women, Forgive me for being dismissive when you expressed yourself. I didn't respect your feelings.**

1. How do you feel when your voice is silenced?

_____

_____

_____

_____

2. How have you responded to this type of behavior? How was your response received?

_____

_____

_____

_____

3. What do you need to release yourself from the pain caused by these actions?

_____

_____

_____

_____

Dear Black Women, Forgive me for believing that as a man, I am better than you. I realize that without you there is no me.

1. Have you ever been treated as less than because you are a woman? How did you feel?

_____

_____

_____

_____

2. How have you responded to this type of behavior? How has your response been received?

_____

_____

_____

_____

3. How could this realization assist with the overall interactions between Black men and Black women?

_____

_____

_____

_____

# Questions:
# Because Self-Reflection is Healthy

Dear Black Women, When was the last time you were accepted for who you are?

Share what you feel:

_____

_____

_____

_____

_____

_____

_____

_____

_____

_____

_____

# Dear Black Women,
What are some of the burdens that you carry as a Black woman?

Share what you feel:

_____

_____

_____

_____

_____

_____

_____

_____

_____

_____

_____

# Dear Black Women,
What beliefs do you hold about yourself? Where do those beliefs come from?

Share what you feel:

_____

_____

_____

_____

_____

_____

_____

_____

_____

_____

_____

Dear Black Women, When you look in the mirror, what do you see?

Share what you feel:

_____

_____

_____

_____

_____

_____

_____

_____

_____

_____

_____

Dear Black Women, When did you learn to love and accept your body?

Share what you feel:

_____

_____

_____

_____

_____

_____

_____

_____

_____

_____

_____

_____

# Dear Black Women, What is self-love? How is it expressed in your life?

Share what you feel:

_____

_____

_____

_____

_____

_____

_____

_____

_____

_____

_____

**Dear Black Women,
What does love from another person look like to you?**

Share what you feel:

_____

_____

_____

_____

_____

_____

_____

_____

_____

_____

_____

# Dear Black Women, What has fear prevented you from expressing?

Share what you feel:

_____

_____

_____

_____

_____

_____

_____

_____

_____

_____

_____

_____

# Dear Black Women,
How important is being heard & understood without judgement?

Share what you feel:

_____

_____

_____

_____

_____

_____

_____

_____

_____

_____

_____

_____

**Dear Black Women,**
**What are some of the pressures that you face but rarely talk about?**

Share what you feel:

_____

_____

_____

_____

_____

_____

_____

_____

_____

_____

_____

Dear Black Women, What were you taught about relationships when you were young? How did it help or hinder you?

Share what you feel:

_____

_____

_____

_____

_____

_____

_____

_____

_____

_____

_____

**Dear Black Women,**
**What were you**
**taught about**
**your sexuality**
**as a young girl?**
**How did that**
**influence your**
**thoughts and**
**perceptions?**

Share what you feel:

_____

_____

_____

_____

_____

_____

_____

_____

_____

_____

_____

_____

# Dear Black Women,
What are or has been your greatest challenges in relationships?

Share what you feel:

_____

_____

_____

_____

_____

_____

_____

_____

_____

_____

_____

_____

**Dear Black Women,
How has your upbringing molded you into the person you are today?**

Share what you feel:

_____

_____

_____

_____

_____

_____

_____

_____

_____

_____

_____

Dear Black Women,
Who do you need to forgive in order to begin to heal?

Share what you feel:

_____

_____

_____

_____

_____

_____

_____

_____

_____

_____

_____

# Affirmations:
# Because Encouragement
# is Nourishing

Dear Black
Women,
It is an honor
and a privilege
to love you.

1. Describe what you feel when you read this statement.

_____

_____

_____

_____

2. How open are you to receiving this type of love & appreciation?

_____

_____

_____

_____

3. How do you or would you feel knowing that someone realizes that it is an honor & a privilege to love you?

_____

_____

_____

_____

**Dear Black Women, Being everything to everyone is not your responsibility.**

1. Describe a time when you put someone else's needs before your own when you really didn't want to.

_____

_____

_____

_____

2. What drives you to want to please others at the cost of yourself?

_____

_____

_____

_____

3. How would it feel to establish boundaries that honor who you are and increase your peace of mind?

_____

_____

_____

_____

**Dear Black Women, Give yourself permission to REST.**

1. Describe a time when you needed to rest, but didn't make the time to do so. What was going through your mind?

_____

_____

_____

_____

2. How often do you sacrifice your time to rest to do something else that "has to get done"?

_____

_____

_____

_____

3. How would prioritizing rest benefit your life?

_____

_____

_____

_____

# Dear Black Women, I Respect You.

1. Describe the importance of respect in your life.

_____

_____

_____

_____

2. Do you feel respected as a Black woman?

_____

_____

_____

_____

3. How do you show yourself respect?

_____

_____

_____

_____

Dear Black Women,
You are one of a kind. There is no need to compare yourself to anyone else.

1. What do you feel when you read this
statement?

_____

_____

_____

_____

2. Describe a time when you compared yourself to
someone else? What feelings did you
experience?

_____

_____

_____

_____

3. How could your life change if you truly
believed this statement?

_____

_____

_____

_____

# Dear Black Women, I Believe in You.

1. When's that last time someone said this to you?

_____

_____

_____

_____

2. When's the last time you believed in yourself?

_____

_____

_____

_____

3. How do you feel when you know someone
genuinely believes in you?

_____

_____

_____

_____

**Dear Black Women,
Your intuition is always on point. Filter out the noise and listen.**

1. How often do you listen to your intuition (your internal knowing)?

_____

_____

_____

_____

2. What are the benefits to being aligned with your intuition?

_____

_____

_____

_____

3. What could you do to be in greater alignment with your intuition? How could that improve your quality of life?

_____

_____

_____

_____

Dear Black
Women,
I accept you as
you are.

1. When's that last time someone said this to you?

_____

_____

_____

_____

2. Do you accept yourself as you are?

_____

_____

_____

_____

3. What do you feel when you know someone
genuinely accepts you?

_____

_____

_____

_____

Dear Black Women, Never be afraid to clearly communicate your wants, needs, & desires.

1. Describe a time when you felt afraid to communicate your wants, needs, and desires.

_____

_____

_____

_____

2. What was the result of not clearly communicating? How did you feel?

_____

_____

_____

_____

3. How could clearly communicating your wants, needs, and desires improve your quality of life?

_____

_____

_____

_____

Dear Black Women, It's okay to cry. Releasing your feelings and stress through tears is a part of the human experience.

1. What were you taught about crying as a child?

_____

_____

_____

_____

2. How did your childhood teachings help or hinder you when expressing the range of your emotions?

_____

_____

_____

_____

3. When's the last time you allowed yourself to cry?

_____

_____

_____

_____

Dear Black Women, Having unconditional love for yourself is more important than the love you receive from others. Love you first.

1. What are the benefits of loving yourself?

_____

_____

_____

_____

2. How does self-love manifest itself in your life?

_____

_____

_____

_____

3. In what areas can you improve the way you
love yourself?

_____

_____

_____

_____

Dear Black Women, Tell the little girl in you that you love her.

Take some time to write a letter to your younger self. When did she need love? When did she need to know it wasn't her fault? When did she need to know she would be okay? What else could have helped her?

_____

_____

_____

_____

_____

_____

_____

_____

_____

_____

_____

_____

Dear Black Women, Forgive Yourself. Carry the lesson, not the pain.

1. What keeps you from forgiving yourself?

_____

_____

_____

_____

2. How does your lack of forgiveness of yourself affect other areas of your life?

_____

_____

_____

_____

3. In what ways can your life improve if you were willing to forgive yourself?

_____

_____

_____

_____

# Dear Black Women, Take time to celebrate YOU!

1. You are a multi-faceted human being! How are you celebrating the fullness of you?

_____

_____

_____

_____

2. Describe a time when you took time to celebrate yourself. How did you feel?

_____

_____

_____

_____

3. What are benefits of taking time out to celebrate who you are and what you have accomplished?

_____

_____

_____

_____

# Dear Black Women, I'm proud of you.

1. When was the last time someone you love and respect told you that they were proud of you?

_____

_____

_____

_____

2. When was the last time you were proud of yourself?

_____

_____

_____

_____

3. What do you feel when these words are said to you with authenticity?

_____

_____

_____

_____

Dear Black Women, You are not alone. Your Divine Source is with you always. Stay connected.

1. How often do you feel like you are alone in life?
Where does that feeling come from?

_____

_____

_____

_____

2. How often are you connecting with your Divine
Source (add the name that feels right to you)?

_____

_____

_____

_____

3. How could your quality of life improve by
 creating a practice in which this is a priority?

_____

_____

_____

_____

**Dear Black Women,**
**Be patient with yourself. You're on your own path, growing at your own pace, and that's okay.**

1.How are you showing yourself patience?

_____

_____

_____

_____

2. What are some benefits of taking your time to grow at your own pace?

_____

_____

_____

_____

3. How could your quality of life improve if you were patient with yourself and your journey?

_____

_____

_____

_____

# Afterword

We are so happy that you made it through this healing tool. Take time to celebrate your accomplishment! Take in what you have learned about yourself. Healing isn't an easy task, but it's necessary and continuous.

If you've had a positive experience with this book, please write a review on Amazon. There are Black women all over the world looking for tools to help them on their healing journey. Will you help point them in this direction?

We are so grateful to you!

# Stay Connected

Join the Dear Black Women Private Group on Facebook:

https://bit.ly/3bRryCR

Follow Jewel Guy on IG: @jewelguy.co
Follow Desmond Guy on IG: @such_iz_lyfe_

# Additional Publications
## Sold at www.jewelguy.co/shop

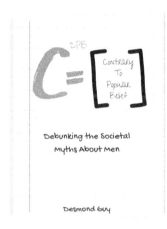

Contrary to Popular Belief:
Debunking the Societal Myths About Men
(Paperback & Ebook)

Dear Black Men: Affirmations, Questions,
& Apologies You May Not Have Heard
(Paperback & Ebook)

Show Your Love
A photo-documentary series capturing the
candid love stories of 40+ Black Couples.
(Ebook)

CPSIA information can be obtained
at www.ICGtesting.com
Printed in the USA
BVHW060908250321
603396BV00008B/643

9 781034 599227